KU-540-152

FOUR GATES OF LOTHIAN

and other poems

With the author's Compliments

Forbes Macgregor

10/12/80

BY THE SAME AUTHOR:

SCOTS PROVERBS AND RHYMES

Moray Press, 1948
W. & R. Chambers, 1970
Pinetree Press, 1976

DORIC SPICE

Blackford Press, 1956
Pinetree Press 1960

GOWKS OF MOWDIEKNOWES

Pinetree Press, 1963

WHAT IS EDUCATION IN SCOTLAND

Akros, 1970

MACGREGOR'S MIXTURE

Gordon Wright, 1976

CLAN GREGOR

Clan Gregor Society, 1977

FOUR GATES OF LOTHIAN
and other poems

1921—1978

By

FORBES MACGREGOR

Selected and Introduced

by

Alastair Mackie

Published by
FORBES MACGREGOR
17 Kaimes Road, Edinburgh EH12 6JS
SCOTLAND

1979

ISBN O 9506348 0 8

Cover design by Jean Macgregor

Author's photograph by Gordon Wright

Printed in Scotland by
D. MACDONALD LTD.
29 Albany Street, Edinburgh EH1 3QN

The great garden of poetry where there are no forbidden fruits.

Victor Hugo.

CONTENTS

INTRODUCTION

Friends and acquaintances of Forbes Macgregor are widely aware that he has been around for a long time. He was one of the small band of young Scots, like MacDiarmid and Albert Mackie, who sat at the feet of that rare schoolmaster George Ogilvie, in the early days of the Scots Renaissance.

It is therefore fitting that this volume of his work covering over half a century should now be offered to the public. Macgregor has no illusions about his literary status; he will, I think, agree that this collection reveals him to be an accomplished, witty, and irreverent—thank God—craftsman of many kinds of light verse, a pasticheur of quality and in one or two poems a lyric poet. Macgregor however can never resist the comic spirit from breaking into his inspiration. To do otherwise would cut against the witty grain that permeates his sensibility.

In this collection the discerning reader will find a variety of work in a variety of traditional forms to "gust his gab," to use an excellent Scots phrase from Fergusson. For Forbes Macgregor has a wide and fluent mastery of Scots which may open the eyes of those unfamiliar with his work. Let them taste the uproarious bawdry of "Kittlenakit Hop" or "Hogmanay" and judge the truth of this. I know I have laughed out loud at the high jinks of such pieces—something I rarely do with the bulk of so-called comic verse. They should be prime poems in any future anthology in this genre.

Here then are bawdy ballads and songs, bubbling occasional verse, immodest parodies and also lyrics veined with a love of the country spaces of the Border and their evocative place-names.

"Non omnis moriar" wrote Horace of his work. Nor do I think that one or two poems in this book will "wholly die" either. Their laughter deserves to last.

ALASTAIR MACKIE.

7

AILLIE BELCHIE

O, Bunkle, Billie, and Blanerne,
The like again ye'll never see
For Aillie Belchie's brocht to bairn
For a' she's drooned her eldest three.

O, whatna weird will be in store
For Aillie Belchie's fourth-born babe?
There's little doot the hardened whore
Will cuist it in the Leigate Lade.

As I gaed doon by Billie Mire
Aboot the mirkest oor o nicht
I saw three pouks wi powes on fire;
'Twas weel I wot a ferlie sicht.

"Dear brethren twain," the sister said,
Though twa weeks auld she couldna be,
"Oor mither's brocht again to bed,
But noo the twa o them shall dee."

And sae it fell as she foreknew
As Beltane Day begood to daw
That Aillie Belchie took a grew
And lang or nicht she soughed awa.

They held her wake as weel's they micht
Wi bannock breid and barley yill:
By fower-and-twenty cannle-licht
They sate them doon wi richt guidwill.

The Bunkle nock had chappit twa
And Droedan's ghaist wheenged in his lair:
Folk thocht nae hairm that Elder Shaw
Should lead an exorceese wi prayer.

"O, Lord, hae mercy on a' such
As Thou hast gaithered here and fed
And no forgettin yon damned bitch
That lies stark-deid upon the bed."

9

"For she has drooned her bastards three
Afore they were kirstened to salvation,
And sinned to the nineteenth degree,
And maybe mair, o fornication."

They buried her doon in the Lintlaw Haugh
Atween an ash and an auld bourtree
And up frae her grave sprang a sabbin saugh
Where ay in Mey sing linties three.

BENAIAH BOWDER

Tom Bowdler's god-child, lucky lad,
Was far removed from influence bad;
His snow-white, silken, christening ribbon
Assumed twixt Shakespeare's Works and Gibbon.

The very reverend Bowdler, Tom,
Being anxious to preserve him from
The least suggestion of all evil
And keep his god-child from the D —— l,

Deliberated ere too late,
The "l" in's name t'eradicate,
And so, before his first b — m-powder
He christened him Benaiah Bowder.

But man is sinful and his frame
Conforms to nature, and the blame
Rests with our primal curse, 'tis said;
Without remorse babes p —— s the bed.

Or, if with purgative most mild
The mother fond doth dose her child
Can she repine when half the night
He wallows in a slough of s —— e?

But ere his second year was sped
More Christian ethics filled his head
And, if he deemed these texts a farce,
He earned, and got, a well-whipt a —— e.

And so Benaiah, strictly bred,
And on the purest Gospel fed,
Was 'listed in a famous college
Without a stain of c——l knowledge.

Then to his horror he found out
Th' establishment of Doctor Stout
Had scarce as pure a one as he
But openly they'ld s —— t and p —— e.

11

Ben soon admonished such behaviour
And told these louts of their blest S —— r;
His pains were execrably paid
With foul ex —— ta on him laid.

At length to puberty he grew
Which brought temptations not a few;
He heard strong oaths like H—ll and G—dd—m,
Sins of G —— h and of S —— m.

In time he gained a well-earned place
In Oxford, where a pious race
Conspired to get a good degree
By studying Div —— ty.

But in that flock of snow-white lambs
There were a few black well-hung rams
Who swore by Castor and by Pollux
They'ld get a wench to cool their b —— ks.

In Holy Writ each sought a text
Lest his nice conscience should be vext;
His argument to cover that
Was thick as old King David's t —— t.

Benaiah met a pious maid,
High Church, to all appearance staid;
Who frowned on gambling, drinking, kissing,
And blushed to see a dog a-p —— g.

This prudish damsel had offended
The chamber-maid that on her tended:
For spite, her d —— rs with itching powder
She dusted, ere she met Ben Bowder.

On spiritual bliss they prated,
Then High Church matters Miss debated;
Desire came on her with a rush;
She cried, "O, sir, pray scratch my b —— h!"

12

Benaiah, willing to comply,
Slid his right hand along her t —— h:
They fell together to the floor
And f —— d for full three hours and more.

So all Tom Bowdler's high endeavour
One wench's trick had wrecked forever,
But Ben to set the balance right
F —— d maid and mistress all that night.

BIRD-SANG IN STRATHCLYDE

Ae day in Lammas as I gaed
Laigh doon on Campsie Fell,
A-gaitherin o blaeberries,
I cam upon a dell.
The air was close and hingy,
The flees in foorichs flew,
A wee taet weary I sate doon
For blaeberries were few.

The wid was dern and rosetty,
Scots firs stude straucht and hie,
Fankled wi brammles, birsled whins,
A bit aboon the brie.
It aince had been a quarry-hole
Howkt oot o Campsie-side,
The kinna bosky bieldy bit
Whaur gangrel bodies bide.

Deep doon amang the breckan strae,
Melled in wi dry-dyke stanes,
Were twa crackt pats o Carron cast,
A wheen o auld blaired banes;
Taids' feet serred weel their puddock kytes,
For fifty year or mair
Had passed, sin it had been their wytes
To skail some tinker's fare.

I sate and wonnert to mysel,
A' in the bird-thrang wid,
Whit tide o kailpat fortune flowed
To cuist them here at flude.
I heard alang the bosky raw
The wran and robin kythe,
The houlet and the hoodie-craw.
The merle and mavis blythe.

14

The merle and the mavis,
The robin and the wran,
The houlet and the hoodie-craw,
Syne spak wi tongues o man.
But ilk ane kept its ain leid,
Wran and robin chirmed thegither,
The merle was a furthy chiel,
The mavis was a blether,
The lang-lugged houlet hooed and haughed
But the craw krecked in a' weather.

The Robin and the Wran

Wran (tremolo):Therra perra verra roostie Jerra helmets.
Robin (vibrato): Wherra perra roostie Jerra helmets?
Wran: Ower hearr irra cennerr orra quarra.
Robin: Rerrnaw blurra roostie Jerra helmets.
Wran: Wharr arra gin rerrnaw aperra Jerra helmets?
Robin: Rerra perra airn jerraboams.
Wran: Nawrerrnaw, reer muckle bigger norra jerra.
Robin: Aye, rerr muckle bigger norra jerra.
Wran: Rerr mair liker forra bea perra airn parritch pingles.
Robin: Noo ye serrit.   Therra perra pingles.
Wran: Ravegoat hannles bittrae hannagoat naeerrses.
Robin: Wha wad wanna gaw an brekkrae pingles?
Wran: Wharra shemmye dinna hae yer fairrer's barra.
Robin: Fairrer's barra's ower narra forra pingle.
Wran: Gin rerrnaw awa ramarra we kin borra fairrer's lorra.
Robin: Weasle commagen ramarra wirra lorra.
                (Exeunt Robin and Wran)

15

The Mavis and the Merle

Merle (In Kelvinside tetrameters): Mavis, will you fill the kettle while I light the picnic fire?

Mavis (In King's Park repetitives): Do be careful.   Yes, be careful. The woods are dry.   Terribly dry.

Merle: That's all right, dear.   I'll keep trying not to light your funeral pyre.

Mavis: My, you're sarky.   Even narky.

Merle: Well, it's no fun fondling Twiggies when your hands are full of Jag.

Mavis: O, my dear.   Come over here.   I'll try to pull them out.   Now be a brave Boy Scout.   All gone, all gone. Mummy kiss it, make it better.

Merle: What are these things in the bracken just beside the cooky bag?

Mavis: My, they're pots.   Old iron pots.   Victorianas.   Loud hosannas.   Won't they look well filled with ferns?   We'll be upsides with the Nairns.

Merle: Just the old junk we were needing to complete our happy day.

Mavis: They look so authentic.   Your mum will be frentic. They're functional.   They're functional.

Merle: How can they fulfil a function when their bottoms are away?

Mavis: O, how vulgar.   Don't be vulgar.   Say heels.   Say heels. Or soles, yes, soles.

Merle: You're conveniently forgetting what your cousin Jack would say.

Mavis: But he's different.   He's a sailor.   He's a jolly old Jack Tar.   And you know what sailors are.   Or do you?   Yes, do you?

Merle: I don't like your imputation that I'm just a kind of pouf.

Mavis: O, really, o, really.   That's the end.   That's the end. I'm going home now, home now.   Such talk I've never heard.   What's the meaning of that word?   Unspeakable. Unrepeatable.   O, when shall I recapture my first fine careless rapture?

(Exeunt Mavis and Merle)

16

The Houlet and the Craw

Craw (Corvus Corone): Are ye there, Miss Otus Houlet, are ye
    there?
Houlet (Strix Otus): Aye, I'm cooerin in my booer in the sauch.
Craw: Did ye hear yon pauchly craturs frae the toon?
Houlet: Aye, I kenna hoo they didna gar ye lauch.
Craw: Lauch? I gey near shook the poolies frae my croon.
Houlet: Div ye think they'll come and tak oor airn quaichs?
Craw: Gin they ettle I'll sune fley them wi a "Kauch!"
Houlet: I wad gar them lowp the haugh there wi my skraighs.
Craw: Div ye mind yon mauchy nicht the pots were brocht?
Houlet: Div I no? Thon drucken pauchles wi their waar.
Craw: The wheech o their bauch crowdie garred me bock.
Houlet: Yet the clairty cailliach cairds begood to narr.
Craw: Like twa hungry tykes they ruggit ower a crock.
Houlet: Syne they skailed their dauchy crowdie ower the lowe.
Craw: Then they focht wi airn nicht-couls in the mirk.
Houlet: And wi stanes crackt baith the pots upon their powe.
Craw: Syne they slept and snored like beylies in a kirk.
Houlet: Hoo! Hoo! Hoo! Hagh! Keevit!
Craw: Kraar! Kraar!
                (Exeunt Craw and Houlet)

      And a gowk or a ghaist,
      Cried on the hill:
      "Cw? Cw? Myn ghu?"
      Then a' was still.

17

BLACK FRIDAY

O, weary winter rains that fa
To mell wi bree o Lammer snaw,
Gae seepin, seepin doon.
Let Waitch rin on to mossy Dye
And creep black Billiemire to Eye
But to my love gae doon.
Aneath the foonds o Sodger's Law
Laigh atween Hurker and Craig Taw
It's ay green, green at noon
Where lie my true-love's tuim ee-banes
Brichter than feak-rock chuckie-stanes
And blinner than the moon.
A curse o Rammel's thunnerin bay
That brak his stoot rig-bane in twae
Afore he'd leave to droon.
The last o eird that e'er he saw
Was through the haar the wild Doolaw
Blae lichtnin ower its croon.
O fair and fause thon Thursday's eve;
O, black the Friday's daw I grieve
That weedowed hauf the toon.
O, weary rain and wintry shooer
Through the airn hert o Lammermuir
Gae seepin, seepin doon.
O, mell ye wi the laighest wave;
Say, through his bairn's unkirstened grave,
His true-love sends ye doon.

18

TO CASSANDRA
(from Ronsard)

Unto yon rose, my dear, at the garden's end
Our steps this eventide we'll gently wend,
O'er shady lawn the haunt of muses nine
Where, lover-leaning, arm in clinging arm,
I sighed this morn at all her purple charm
And kissed alike her silk-soft lips and thine.

Alas, she has but barely sighed for love
Of being, when she is no more above.
Cruel, cruel, o Nature; hast thou harshly torn
Her beauties? Then thou art in truth a churl
Who from her throne this queen of love wouldst hurl
That she should die at night who's crowned at morn.

Straight from my heart, my dear, comes this
That I would say to thee. Seize thou the bliss
Of verdant youth and tender-opening love;
Haste thee nor hesitate, this God-given day,
Thy youth as roses' fast doth fade away;
No flower so beautiful but time doth prove.

CLARTY KIRSTAN

The bailie's wife o Bite-aboot
She was a steerin hizzy,
She wrocht and dirled the shite aboot
Till a' the lads were dizzy.

Chorus:
And ay richt merrily she'd sing
As through the sharn she'd ploiter,
"There's naething beats a standing thing,
Lay on, lads, dinna loiter!
The sun's no up but the nicht is gane,
Coup your corn and pay your kain,
Wark to fill your hungry wame,
Piss and gang to bed again."

She milked the kye wi sharny neives
And then she kirned the butter,
And Clarty Kirstan's hame-made cheese
Gied Hielandman the skitter.

She didna loe a bonny lass,
Quo she, "It's gey weel kenned
Hooever braw ye are ye'll pass
To coo-shites in the end."

She clotched amang the pairs o horse
Cled but in flannen goonie,
Her serk-tail kiltet to the erse,
Her wame a sicht for ony.

Clarty Kirstan, think ye shame,
What though ye coup them corn,
To shaw the naigs your dirty wame
And gie the lads the horn.

Syne frae her bed she skraighet ben,
The clarty shameless limmer;
"Hey, Geordie Broon, to piss I'm fain,
Gae rax me up the chaumer."

20

Noo, Geordie was a shamefast chiel;
His first thocht was to brain her:
"But na," thocht he, "the clarty deil,"
And handed her the strainer.

The bailie gied a snortin snore
Ye micht hae heard at Kelsae
Just as his wife, the clarty whore,
Pissed splairgin through the milsey.

"O, Kirstan, Kirstan, haud within,
Your twatt's grown ower vaunty:
Guid faith, I'm droukit to the skin;
Ye've gane and missed the shanty."

COMPLAINT ON A SCHOOL DINNER
in General Assembly Week, 1964

O thou, wha Commissaries guide,
Let me intil thy lug confide
A secret that I'd raither hide
Aboot oor denner—
It may hae gien ye muckle pride—
It garred me scunner.

Nae doot th' Assembly's gaithered here
Wi psalm and paraphrase and prayer
To castigate the nation sair
On its misdeeds
Or fling oot texts and never spare
Upon oor heids.

But guidsakes, sir, that's nocht but talk,
The meenisters maun hae their crack,
There was nae need for ye to ac'
Upon a text
And send the bairns oot sic hard tack
As hae them vext.

Lord kens we've had dry meat afore
But this was saut as Sodom's shore;
We curst your basket and your store
O' rice and raisin,
I thocht we'd had coo's milk galore
This summer season.

I ken fu weel what text ye saw
To gie the bairns sic belly-thraw,
Ezekiel thretty-seiven and twa,
Just like your pie,
Or banes that blaired on Israel's shaw,
"They were gey dry."

CYMRIC FASTNESS

Mocking day yon hornéd moon
Gleams copper over Gwynion,
Where I stand on August eve
By Gala lone and pensive,
Hating yet you hornéd host,
Sea-wolves of Wodin foremost,
Twice thrown down from Gwynion fort
To sleep sound with false comfort
Of Valhalla, vermin slain
By war-hounds of Gododdin.

Plainly I see nine stars shine,
Sky still red o'er Dineiddyn.
Owls now rouse themselves to sing,
To float like down, a-mousing.
Now, strange cry so late to hear
From June's feathered harbinger,
"Cuckoo? Cuckoo?" the woods ring,
Though he's hoarse with vain questing
All summer long in green glades
Of birch, or by hill cascades.
Filling quiet woods with such din,
He may well be mad Myrddin;
"Cruelly slain because of me,"
Crying "where are the Cymri?"
Mad bird, those you seek are dead,
You yourself soon benighted,
Caught up in thorns and briars,
Lost in Gala's meanders.

Hear water-ouzel's shrill note,
His snowy-girdled waistcoat
To some dry perch in fir-tree
Through shades will guide you safely;
But of lost Cymri less trace
Than last year's snow in crevice
That's not from summer sun hid
On Dindreich loved of druid.
Melted, too, starred garlic's frost,
Emblem of Cymri; whitest
Of flowers in pale bulb wait,
Dreaming of spring, hibernate.

23

No longer through dim woods flit
But perch now, restless spirit;
Wake with chilly wraiths of dawn
And bide an hour on Gwynion
Where despite all past distress
Cymri cling to this fastness.

Mountain pansy's yellow star
Glints gold hair of Gwenhwyfar;
Elfin rhymes of Gogledd ring
From choirs of heart's-ease smiling:
Borne away from satyr bees
In fleet leafy pinnaces,
Hainberry nymphs, sweet as frail,
Shy in silken pannicle;
When their fruiting time has come
No more remembered perfume
Lambent thuribles distil
Than these in sylvan temple.
Chalice harebells, blue and white,
Holding draughts of pale sunlight,
Tell of wine and meddyglyn
Poured forth in high Dineiddyn;
Mead soon soured to bitter gall
In throes of Catraeth's battle;
Dearly bought mead in death's hour;
Youth in years, men in valour,
Three score and three hundred slain,
Three returned to Dineiddyn.

Bourtree that black berries bears
In shires of Frisian strangers,
Mourning over Owain dead
Here spurts her fruit, heart's blood-red.

Rowan's fragrant bloom like snow
At noon melts, leaves no shadow;
Early berries, bitter red,
From evil keeping homestead;
Arthur, by Medraut undone,
Untimely slain at Camlann;
Of the Cymri warriors king,
Sweetest flower, brief blooming.

24

DECIMALISATION

Homo sapiens
With his prehensile tens,
His grasping digital paw,
Holds the world in awe:
Ten are his god's commands
The centuries throughout
To those millennial lands
Where myriads shout,
"Hallelujah! Homo Sapiens!"
And wave celestial, still prehensile tens.

DYING TESTAMENT OF A VICTORIAN PHYSICIST

When in my last home you have pressed
My body, and my soul goes free,
My ghost shall do its level best
To disprove relativity.

In vain shall Morley-mirrors cast
Their light-rays, to prove Newton wrong;
My ghost shall turn iconoclast
And push the tardy rays along.

As a recurring decimal,
Or a redundant surd,
I'll haunt their calculations all
And give their hopes the bird.

Or as an ultra-violet,
That's born to blush unseen,
I'll jigger up their spectrum set
And prove their alpha green.

Approaching constellations bright,
I'll swim into their lenses
Who'ld put the nebulae to flight,
These Larmors and Lorentzes.

The baleful light that seen to blaze
O'er Wilson at the sun's eclipse
Won't be a faint galactic haze
But curses from my lips.

When all lines are proved circular
By logic, or Mah Jong,
I'll drop quite perpendicular
To Hell, and prove them wrong.

26

ERSEHOLE O' CREATION

I bade fareweel to my dearie
And I herdit at Blaweary
Up the muirlands in the hert o' desolation;
The mistress she was crabbie
Sae I sune agreed wi Rabbie
I was bidin up the ersehole o' creation.

The yowes were yeld and scabbit
But could lowp dykes like a rabbit
And the dochters o' the hoose were nae temptation;
The meat and cheese was mawkie
And the farls were soor as cackie
Which was likely up the ersehole o' creation.

The braes were thrang wi edders
And they yokit on the wedders;
There was rime and snaw a' year withoot cessation;
Sae as quick's a lintie shitin
I did a munelicht flittin,
The richt wey to leave the ersehole o' creation.

FIFTY PENCE PIECE, NEW-MINTED

Roll or totter, infant still,
Through the fruit-machine or till,
In this hippy age a hep—
tagonal exchange for pep;
You will still be in your prime
When I'm well past spending time,
Yet I'll make my grimace teethy
As I'm ferried over Lethe;
On the oboli you'll clang
With a rich Britannic bang;
From my viewpoint o'er the river
Forward, forward may you range,
Spinning with seven bobs forever
Down the ringing grooves of change.

FOUR GATES OF LOTHIAN

Who goes out by the North Gate,
Out from the land of Loth;
In sun, in cloud, in drought or spate,
Why steals he out by the Northern gate
From the land that brought him forth?

'Tis I go out by the North gate,
I, Esk of briery ways.
Far from the brown-welled hills of home,
From Logan's Crag, Carnethy's dome,
Or gliding silent where the oak
Throws down black-staining leaves to choke
My way to Hawthornden,
I've wandered till at last I meet
The salt sea curling o'er my feet
Beyond the land of men.

Who goes out by the South gate,
Out from the land of Loth;
In sun, in cloud, in drought or spate,
Why steals he out by the Southern gate
From the land that brought him forth?

'Tis I go out by the South gate,
I, Heriot of the Hopes.
From Moorfoots bleak in vast array
Where first the gladdening eastern day
Strikes faint the wounds of Blackhope Scar
And tints the Yarrow Hills afar
I draw my rugged birth;
So, laughing round each hazelled hill,
I wend my devious way, until
In Tweed I drown my mirth.

Who goes out by the East gate,
Out from the land of Loth;
In sun, in cloud, in drought or spate,
Why steals he out by the Eastern gate
From the land that brought him forth?

'Tis I go out by the East gate,
I, Tyne of pleasant meads;
By apple-orchards white as snow,
And quiet green kirkyards I go,
From Ford to haar-swept Tynninghame
Where first the fair-crowned Angles came
Broad-chested from the wave;
So steal I now 'neath wooded hills,
So rush I from your watermills
To be no more your slave.

Who goes out by the West gate,
Out from the land of Loth;
In sun, in cloud, in drought or spate,
Why steals he out by the Western gate
From the land that brought him forth?

There's none go out by the West gate
But I, the gangrel man;
By Cloich beneath the summer moon
And Carlin's Loups where hill pines croon
My road seeks out by syke and howe
Drummelzier's magic hawthorn bough
Where tryst I keep with him
Who talked with Pan in Doric glades
And learned the lore of naiad maids
When all the world was dim.

HAIKAI

Kestrel over Westlinton Kirkyard

Fly on, o falcon,
Great black kite struck long ago,
Seek thy meat elsewhere.

October Gale

Brown leaves and sparrows
Blown by the gale eastward fly
To shelter in droves.

HE WINNA DAE FOR ME

When Sandy comes to tell his mind
Deep wading through the snaw
He is to me a lover kind
The kindest e'er I saw.
When locked within his arms, I'm shair,
Nae lass could happier be
But then, alas, he is sae puir
He winna dae for me.

Noo Tammy comes when spring is nigh
And green is ilka shaw,
He kisses me and gies a sigh
He thinks I am sae braw,
I'm shair he means to gie me sport
I canna happier be,—
But then his john it is sae short,
He winna dae for me.

When simmer days are saft and warm
Sweet Billie comes to woo,
He swears he ne'er will dae me hairm,
I doot it's ower true.
I think it would be grand to sin,
I canna happier be;—
I feel his stanes—he has but yin!
He winna dae for me.

The autumn comes, the wids are broon,
And Bob comes ower the muir,
He cuddles me and lays me doon
And ca's me his wee hure.
Although I ken he winna wed
Until the day I dee
Richt willingly we gang to bed,
He has to dae for me.

HEART OF THE BORDER

The far-off rumble of the thunder dies
Against the sunset beyond Fanna Hill:
Deep in the dale the mists like wraiths arise
O'er Ravenburn and Jed's impetuous rill.
Where dark Peel Fell and brooding Carter fill
The eastern skyline, on oblivion's shore,
The rusted wire-fence of the Border still
Delineates the rivalries of yore.
Faintly across the Catrail runs the score
Pale through the heather, where the Roman road
Hides neath a grassy track for evermore
The quarried stones that Theodosius strode.
These are but cicatrices on the skin;
The heart retains the conflict far within.

HERBERIE

There's naebody comes near my hoose ony mair
But wi fower sic auld friends I've nae need to care.
I've auld whisky to drink, auld timmer to burn,
Auld Scots buiks to read, thir'll weel dae my turn,
And Jock my auld neebour frae ower the hill
Looks in o' a nicht and lang lunts a ticht fill.
I've aye keepit open the auld richt-o'-wey
And the road's clear eneuch till the tail-end o' Mey,
But wi simmer comes siccan a grushy green growth,
O' thrashes and thrissles and nettles there's routh,
O' braikens and dockans and hie bloody-bells
Wi' segs, dashielaggies, that smoor the moss-wells,
And gin, as it's likely, there's been a bit drow
Ye're droukt to the serk as ye come through the howe,
And that's no to speak o' the keds and the clegs
That licht on your lugs or win through to your legs
Or maybes a bykefu o' foggie bum-bees
Or an antran stang-aither that beeks on the screes.
I whiles gie a leuch when I mind o' the day
When a buik-chapman chiel frae the sooth cam my way
Hoo he ettled to cope me a bund mappamoond
Syne he speired gin I kent that the warld was roond.
'Whiles I wonner, they thocht sae when I gaed to schule,
But ye'll fin oot yoursel as ye sclim ower the hill.'
Gey wabbit he set his sweir shanks to the braes
Though Cyclops' his load he was nae Hercules.
He hasna been back. Naeb'dy seeks me nae mair
They wad fain sell their goods but the road is ower sair.
I whiles think that Heeven has come ower to my side
And God's muckle taen up wi the hoose whaur I bide
For the day the Board cam to arrange for the pooer
An ondeemas thunner-spate dang for twa oor.
They haena been back. Then the birth-control clinic
Ca'ed here wi advice; though I'm nae heathen cynic
The Auld Adam rejoiced when Macfarlane's reid bull
Fair wittrous for want o't gaed wud on the hill.
They haena been back. And I speired a gey paul
At a Witness wha soucht me to save my auld saul:
'Gin the Judgement Day breks, for ye say it's near hand,
Will the Trump soond up here, for we're gey far in land?'
He hasna been back. Wha'll neist tirl at my yett?
Yon baney auld baukin? He'll aiblins forget.

34

HERT-EIDENT AIK

Ye wad be mislaird
Gin ye thocht that the gashled aik
That stauns in the dern wid
Like a wrunkled auld shusy
Wi its crom airms
Cled in the pillions o' touch and spunge
Wad fa in the lichtest souch
O' a simmer sich
That wadna bear up a stanel;
Ye wad be fell mislaird.

For e'en the skarnochin o' a yird-blast
Canna brek the teuch hert
O' the smaaest crannie
At the far-end o' its airms
Nae stranger-like than the neb o' a blitter.

And gin it a' fa thegither
Shoogled oot o' the yird
And be happit up in peat-coom and bree
For a thoosand year,
The feerdie frame o' the flaughterer
Will be dirled and stouned to the mergh
Gin he gie it a staive wi his muir-spade.

Yet, while it stauns, a pield tramort,
E'en the scartin o' a wran's weirdie
Micht whurry the ootermost touch o't
Intae flichterin stuff
And the pynour Aprile wesp
Forfochtan wi a wearisome winterin
Chows it into grool
For the waif wa's o' its bink.

35

HOGMANAY

Gin like mysel ye're Embro-bred
And loe a guid-gaun ballant
In auld Scots style aboot the Mile
Whaur ye yince played as callant,
Then hae this gratis. Haun it on
When ye hae read your fill,
But mind the neist to share the feast
'S as canty as yoursel
And wyce this nicht
At Christ's Kirk at the Tron.

Or I gaed up the Canogate
Last Hogmanay but three
I drappit in on Coul MacFinn
To birl his barley-bree.
He stroaned the guid Glen Leevit oot
My gutsy mutchkin intil,
Syne bouksome fu wi fersellin broo
I stachert yont the lintel
No blate that nicht
To Christ's Kirk at the Tron.

As I drew nigh White Horse Close-end.
Guid faith, I heard a neighin;
Far doon the pend, the Deil forfend,
Oor makars' cuddies brayin:
Wud Pegasos was flichterin roun
Scairtin the chimly wa's;
Ilk makar's steed o dowf Dutch leid
To flee had little cause
Eird-fast this nicht
O' Christ's Kirk at the Tron.

Athort the gurly causey-stanes,
Like Slaver Nick's ain galleon,
Queensberry's Ha the neist I saw
That reekt o reestit hallion;

36

Forenent a genocidal lowe
I saw puir Scotland speetit
While eediot Bull wi hungry gull
Drooled gantin aye and greetit
Puir-moothed this nicht
At Christ's Kirk at the Tron.

But noo I hear cauld airn clink
In freindliness no anger
Gey close at hand's the Gowfers' Land
Whaur I wad tarry langer:
Here furthy fieres haud forth in howff
That reeks o drink and baccies,
Cry 'Fore!' to Fate that drives elate
Or sich 'Eheu fugaces!'
For eild this nicht
At Christ's Kirk at the Tron.

The aiker o auld Faither Time
Aboot to rax a dinger
Richt ower my heid near howe-dumb-deid
Like Damacockles' whinger,
The Janus-heidit Tolbooth Nock
Hings ower his quarneld broo;
In ither mood frae I begood
I glunch the auld To'boo
Gey tuim this nicht
O' Christ's Kirk at the Tron.

The Hielands and the Lallans baith
Hae sert it weel wi ludgers;
They wantit ne'er a comfort here
Like ither conscript sodgers,
Wi hempen gravats for their craigs
And for their hose airn gairters,
Wi broth o skink, snaw-bree for drink,
They micht hae had waur quarters
In Hell yon nicht
No Christ's Kirk at the Tron.

37

In Hell am I, foul fiends aroond;
My airms are bund ahint me;
I am Montrose, and bitter brose
I sup when Campbells mint me:
Frae Moray Hoose's balustrades
In bridal gear accoutrit
MacCallein More's auld pentit hure
Spits on me like a futtret
Wi spite this nicht
At Christ's Kirk at the Tron.

A cat-loup aff in Playhoose Close
An awfu hiddy-giddy;
The Unco Guid are seekin bluid
Led on by Albert's widdy,
Wha's heezed for yince her twal-ton dowp
Frae aff the Institution
And 'gin the God-less rantin squad
She seeks sair retribution
For sin this nicht
At Christ's Kirk at the Tron.

I doot but she maun come ill aff
For a' her sancts and polis
And whatna yairds o palins gairds
Her holiest o holies.
Leadin the Players' phalanx there
Her royal ancéstress Marie
In cramosie, her heid held hie,
Her een wi licht camsteerie
Minds ither nichts
At Christ's Kirk at the Tron.

Langsyne she'd scarce her hoose warmed up
And thocht its joys to hansel
When lantern-jaws and hoodie-craws
Wrocht up a soss o gansel.
'The dance gaed through the lichtit ha';
Or lang she's garred repent it
For kindness' pox, gargrugous Knox,
His vengeance on her sklentit
Gey soor this nicht
At Christ's Kirk at the Tron.

38

Withoot a skirl o 'Gardyloo!'
Frae Weir's Close a' thegither
A brimstane wheech o warlock's keigh
Near cowps me in a swither;
Lug-splittin keckles, keisty, coorse,
Twixt carlins' covens cuitrin,
Whaur Ketrail Weir to nae ill sweir
Wi Hell's wark's aye a-fitterin
In dern this nicht
At Christ's Kirk at the Tron.

Ye'ld hardly lippen, near at hand
This synagogue o Satan,
Doon Warld's End Close, a pang-fu posse
For Gabriel's Trump are waitin.
The wauchle o the waggity
Wambles ilk waesome saul,
Sic skellied een ye ne'er hae seen
Sin Samson speired his paul
O' doom yon nicht
At Timnath at the Tron.

Ye'ld think auld Peter had gi'en ower
To them his pooer to bind
Or lowse the wrath o Hell's braid strath
On fushionless mankind.
Here wi curmurrin guts they sit
Picklin an unco rod,
Ilk mair or less a sermon-gless
Bigs sandy-mills wi God
Far ben this nicht
At Christ's Kirk at the Tron.

Noo whatna ferlie dae I see
As I win to the Tron;
A barren muir near twal dauch square
As flet's a barley scone.
But syne spangs oot a deemas hairst
Frae grun that seemed sae yeld
For a' mankind time oot o mind
Are gaithered to be waled
For ay this nicht
At Christ's Kirk at the Tron.

39

There's some for weicht and heicht are gadged
And some for shape and flavour
And some for girth and some for worth
And twa-three for behaviour:
For soor, for sweet, for het, for cauld,
For length o lume and lowp,
For yin that's soond a score are foond
No worth a cannle-dowp
Brunt-oot this nicht
At Christ's Kirk at the Tron.

Noo sic a yollerin and stramash
Thae coontless thoosands set up;
To dozen't doon auld Bob Mahoun
Frae Hell comes on his jet up:
Gash Gabriel then sets his assize
To wale this unhyne bourach,
For yin aboon cuists twenty doon
In Sandy's Sheuch to slorach
In clart this nicht
Frae Christ's Kirk at the Tron.

The magistrates o Embro Toun
In vain cry, 'Ultra Vires!'
The Prince o Nicht gies them a dicht
To doze them aff like peeries.
'Twas no his wyte ilk bailie's kyte
Ten chalders' weicht had slorpit,
Their reestit sauls like partans' spauls
Were forty to the forpit
Black-nebbed this nicht
At Christ's Kirk at the Tron.

E'en Embro's stag* thae thoosand years
That's goved and glunched forenent her
In philapeg noo yokes on Meg
And rowts and rairs ahint her;
His cervine heid's MacDiarmid's ain
A ruttin thirteen-pointer;

* a heraldic sex-change.

40

His ae intent wi nae relent
To mowe her and anoint her
Fu keen this nicht
At Christ's Kirk at the Tron.

She dreids this neesy dominus
Mair nor she did her frustra
That she has tholed, a virgin cauld,
For near twa hunner lustra.
'A mei. Anglois, tanz piz por vos
Sil mei faist uns enfan':
In Norman-French this doited wench
Skraichs oot baith lood and lang
Near rapt this nicht
At Christ's Kirk at the Tron.

But haud, for trinklin frae the Tron
Eird's zero-oor is chappin:
When a's to tine nae 'Auld Lang Syne'
Nor thocht o kindly clappin.
And wi its weicht o sanctly sauls
The pu'pit for rudder
This muckle kirk intil the mirk
Flees aff wi unco whudder;
For space this nicht
Christ's Kirk has quat the Tron.

The Lord wi rowth o latitude
Yince wrocht galactic glory:
He took a whuff o cosmic snuff
And sneeshit extempóre.
A walth o suns and satellites
Wi Einsteins to endite 'em
And muckle deils to fricht the chiels
He breenged ad infinitum
Through space yon nicht
Frae Christ's Kirk at the Tron.

41

And what for why should he no dae
Wi Eird as He's aye mintit
Sin Eve, braw bird, in Eden's yird
The joys o evil pentit.
In some lown stuffy satellite
A hamehald there we'll hain,
An unbruikt race we'll pray for grace
To dae the same again
As aye we did
At Christ's Kirk at the Tron.

Noo a' you folk wha's left on Eird
While some through space are fleein
To mind your stent be aye content
And think na lang o deein.
An ee gets bleerit sune eneuch
That aye glowers through the peep-hole:
The kirk ye weel may like, atweel,
And no ride on the steeple
On hie this nicht
Wi Christ's Kirk frae the Tron.

And sae auld Eird's last Hogmanay
Breks up wi fowth o fechtin
And mony breeks that burst their steeks
Are nane the waur o dichtin;
Twa braid sea-miles frae here to Leith
Tak a' nicht lang to traivel,
Wi canty crack folk veer and tack
While their five senses raivel
Wi drink this nicht
Frae Christ's Kirk at the Tron.

HOLY WILLIE'S PRAYER FOR LESS RAIN

O, Thou, wha drivest doon the rain
Ower Hieland bens or Lowden's plain
Or splairgin doon ilk Glesga drain
Like reamin swats
Fu simmer lang, eneuch to strain
Thy heavenly vats.

Gie heed unto my humble cry
For wastlin breezes, warm and dry,
To sook the drow aff corn and rye
Or the potaties
And I shall praise Thy majesty
That ever great is.

Lord, we acknowledge Thy full store
From which sunshine and rain Ye pour
Or winds that rush wi sic a splore
Ower a' creation;
But yin thing lacketh and no more
And that's discretion.

Lord, if Thou should'st hae rowth o watter
On drouthy China let it blatter,
Thou needst na heed their senseless yatter,
Yon heathen gang,
Though thoosands float it were nae matter
Doon Yangtseyang.

Or on thae sacrileegious Yanks
Wha strauchtened Mississippi's banks,
Gie them a spate will stop their pranks
Frae as far's St. Paul,
But gin Ye wish to earn oor thanks
Spare Puddock-hole.

O, Lord, we ken that folk sin syne
Hae suffert frae this faut o Thine;
Whiles gear and life alike they tine
For Thy foul weather,
But Thou remembrest me and mine
Aboon a' ither.

Though ilka pairish should be druiket
And Ben More in Loch Katrine dookit
O, let na Puddock-hole be bruiket
Beneath Thy licht;
I carena muckle whase corn's stookit
Gin mine's a' richt.

And in return for Thy attention
To a' thae maitters that I mention
I thank Thee for Thy condescension
To tak advice
And hope 'twill no affect my pension
In Paradise.

JEANNIE ANDERSON, MY JO

Jeannie Anderson, my jo, Jean,
To the curling I maun go, Jean,
For the winter's come, the ice is just O.K.
But I'll be faithful to you, darling,
In my fashion,
I'll be faithful to you, darling, in my way.

Frae March until October
Ye ken I'm never sober,
But I'm turning ower a new leaf frae the-day.
But I'll be faithful to you, darling,
In my fashion,
I'll be faithful to you, darling, in my way.

There's a bonspiel doon in Falkirk,
And a supper-dance in Selkirk,
And a visit to a distillery on the Spey.
But I'll be faithful to you, darling,
In my fashion,
I'll be faithful to you, darling, in my way.

There's a ladies' team frae Holland,
And anither yin frae Poland,
And a set o' weel-built dames frae U.S.A.
But I'll be faithful to you, darling,
In my fashion,
I'll be faithful to you, darling, in my way.

I'll be hame in time for supper,
Ye can warm me up my slippers,
For eleeven or twal, or maybe yin or twae,
But I'll be faithful to you, darling,
In my fashion,
I'll be faithful to you, darling, in my way.

KITTLENAKIT HOP

The folk o Kittlenakit
Are a simple sort o folk;
They drink their beer
A' through the year
And dearly like their joke:
They ploo their fields in winter
And they saw them in the spring
And they thank God for their hervest
When their corn they hameward bring
Fu ripe that nicht.

The guid red soil o Berwickshire
They ploo for daily bread
And when day's dune
At set o sun
Gae fartin-fu to bed;
But ance in ilka twalmonth
They bide up the lee-lang nicht
Troop in frae a' the country
And in dancin tak delicht
Fu wild that nicht.

The nicht o Kittlenakit Hop
The-year cam quickly roond,
Frae Lammermoor
Tae auld Hume Tooer
And e'en frae Berwick's Boond,
The lassies and the laddies
The weedows and the wives
And Forest hures in buses
Cam runnin for their lives
Fu keen that nicht.

The Ha' stands in the Netherhaugh
O' Kittlenakit Burn:
There's hills and moors,
No mills and hures,
Whichever wey ye turn;

46

This winter on the dance-nicht
It was twa feet deep in snaw,
'Twas maybe bloody het inside
Ootside 'twas ten below,
Fu cauld this nicht.

Nae polis-office, schule nor kirk,
Nor public-hoose is there,
Nae Sabbath bell,
Nae Heeven, nae Hell,
And naebody to care:
But there's a Wesleyan Chapel,
For short, a W.C.
To cater ane by ane for a'
That like amenity
Genteel this nicht.

There ye find the wycest sayings
That men can ca' to mind
In gems o verse
In Scotch or Erse
Regarding the behind;
Some write, "This seat's ower wide and tall".
Some gie this apt retort,
"A bloody lie, your bum's ower small,
Your bandy legs ower short
To shite this heicht".

And noo we leave sweet Sharon's shed
For Kittlenakit Hop:
We get inside,
They're in their stride,
The Ha's fu to the top:
The wudden wa's are bulgin
Agin the piled-up snaw,
There's Midside Maggie dancin
Wi a dowp like Co'burn Law
Fu big that nicht.

47

There's ane auld lad has lowsed his belt
To gie his erse a blaw;
"O, Willie Weekes
Pu up your breeks
Your shop-door hangs sae low,
I see your belly plainly
Your sporran wi nae belt,
For shame four-score and seiven
To hae a speldered welt
Fu stiff this nicht".

But noo the baund hae jeckets aff
To play the eichtsome reel;
The vera jeests
Stot up, by Chreest,
At ilka Hieland squeal;
They're hoppin erse for elbae
And strippet to the serk,
Folk were never hauf sae yeukie
Kittlin erses in the derk
Fu daft this nicht.

But noo a collieshangie's
Gotten up ower Tammy Scott,
A hardy chiel
Frae Penmanshiel
Wi shouthers like a stot;
He's cowpt a Hawick harlot
A' her length alang the flair
And exposed for a' the warld to see
Her nyloned erse and mair
Fu braw this nicht.

Ye needna think a thing like that
Wad worry Tinkler Mey;
Ance to a Pole
Her mortal soul
She sellt for ane and thrie,
And for a hauf-croon wadger
For she didna gie a fig
Richt on the waitter bailie
She pissed frae Te'iot Brig
Fu hie that nicht.

48

It never happened but the ance
She'd faintit in a fricht
And that was when
Far doon a pend
She'd seen an unco sicht.
A shepherd that had bocht a pup
And pit it in his ballop
Had got gey fu and for a pee
Richt doon the pend did wallop
Fu fast that nicht.

Instead o pu'in oot his lume
He grabbed the collie's paw
And wi relief
Near past belief
He pissed agin the wa,
But Mey wha keekit horror-struck
Fell faintin on the floor
For sic a hairy thing wi claws
She'd never seen afore,
Fu sharp that nicht.

But noo they bring refreshments in
To Kittlenakit Ha',
There's hills o breid
And potted heid
And sausage rolls for a':
Rab Ha' the Chirnside glutton
Sits doon wi slaverin moo;
He chows his breid and slorps his tea
Just like a Polwart soo
Fu fat this nicht.

But aye the weary cry gets up
Amang the aulder folk,
"This modern food's
Nae bloody good,
It's gettin past a joke.
There's naething nooadays sae grand
When pith begins to fail
As yon heaped bowls o buttered pease
They grew in Lauderdale
Fu guid yon nicht.

49

Auld Sandy frae Pishwanton Mill
Cries oot, "I mind them fine;
When I was young
I cairtit dung
And faithered twenty-nine.
I did it a' on buttered pease
Forbye a wheen o fairtin
Which, if you're musical, relieves
The lang dreich miles o cairtin
Fu sweet yon nicht.

Auld Sandy's life's epitome
Is loodly cheered by a';
He did his wark
And didna shirk
To gie Fate blaw for blaw.
If wee John Longbottom's epitaph's
"Ars longa vita brevis,"
Auld Sandy's cairn should be a pile
O' shite as high's Ben Nevis
Fu saft this nicht.

But noo the runnin buffet
Has at lang last a' run oot;
They've drunk mair beer
And whisky here
Than fill the Kyles o Bute;
The hauf o them are fechtin fu
The tither hauf are fain;
They dance the Reel o Tulloch
Till the sweit rins doon like rain
Fu saut this nicht.

And syne the drink begins to talk
In twenty different weys;
Thae dainty flooers
The Forest hures
Start liftin up their claes;
It vexes a' the mairrit wives
Their men should see sic terses,
They cry, "Fie shame, ye Jezebels,
To show your hawkit erses,
Fu reid this nicht".

50

This rooses up the Forest hures
And stirs their Border blood;
Thae dainty Jills
Frae Te'iot's mills
Let loose an awfu flood:
The choicest words upon their tongues
Fly a' weys hugger-mugger,
Sic as, "Steek up your wizened erse
Ye gundy-gutted buggar".
Fu coorse this nicht.

At last the whisky, tea and beer
Has foond oot where their twatt is:
Folk leave the floor
And seek the door
To dreep their weel-biled tatties:
And syne across the munelicht snaw
They stroan like dugs or kye
And leave as straicht a line there
As the north-west coast o Skye
Fu squint this nicht.

There was ane lass o a' the thrang
That widna piss on snaw;
"There's nocht but gerss
Shall dicht ma erse,
To the privy I maun go".
She bares her dainty bottom,
The frostit frame she feels,
And gey near rigor mortis
Sticks oot stilettoed heels
Fu sharp this nicht.

The first and neediest o the lads
In through the door he cuts,
But Lily's legs
Like hurdle pegs
They ram him in the guts;
He shites hissel wi agony,
He swears he's killed, by Harry,
"And whit a stippet place," cries he
"To keep a bloody barry."
Fu sair this nicht.

51

And sae auld Kittlenakit Hop
Breks up wi fechts an roarin;
It's past midnicht
But till daylicht
Folk tire theirsels wi hurin:
For fifteen miles frae here to Dunse
They spew up a' God's mercies
And leave in ilka wreath o snaw
The print o cowpit erses
Fu plain this nicht.

LOWDEN LASS

Beneath Carnethie's darknin heicht
Where horned sheep ower the moorland pass
And hoodies wing their craikin flicht
'Tis there that bides my Lowden Lass.

It canna be but that the blast
That blaws sae dour agin my name
Will ae day drap and syne be past
And I'll be guidet hame.

Ance mair I'll wear me roond the bend
The loanin maks by Lowdenburn,
I'll hear the sangs that ance I kenned
Frae daffin lasses roond the kirn.

And I will gang by Woodhooselee
And gin the day be bricht and clear
I'm shair I canna help but see
The wee hoose-end that is sae dear.

I'll lowp the burn at Flatterstane,
Win in by dowie Rullion Green,
Sclim Lawheid Hill and ance again
Run whistlin doon the brae to Jean.

But o, the thoucht is muckle mair
Than I can stand, I maun but bide
Till fortune is nae langer sair
But maks my Lowden Lass my bride.

MACLEAN THE CIRCUS POWNIE
(from the Dutch of Edmond de Clercq)

Mair dowf on eird there isna ony
Nor wee MacLean the circus pownie,
Wha on the sawins o his flair
Maun dree his weird for evermair.
Ay by his side there hings a bell
That ca's him frae his crampet cell,
But a' the time he's sair hame-seik;
Oot-through the stable lantron's reek
He sees the unhained Hieland glen
He brookt or he was glaikt by men.
His turn is ower; clowns, claps; plumes flicher;
He gets his pey, a taet o sucker.
O God, be witness to this wean,
The doon-borne circus-horse MacLean.

ON CEMENTING LEVEL THE STABLE FLOOR AT THE OLD MANSE, ANSTRUTHER WESTER, ST. SWITHIN'S DAY, 1963

Bored with his stall, wanting he knew not what,
The minister's gelding chafed here at his lot;
Till his old age from that he was a foal
His stamping hoof ground out this shallow hole.

With more success, penned in my cramping pew,
My soul has raged against the canting crew
And those splenetic kicks I could not quell
Have cut me out a hole as deep as hell.

PHALLATELY FOR JOHNNIE KNOX

There's some speak weel o Johnnie Knox
And hear nae word agin him.
His doctrine was fell orthodox,
Nae semi-breve or minim
Defiled the paraphrase or psalm
His congregation droned oot;
His was the richt to save or damn
When hellfire Johnnie stroaned oot.

But some speak ill o Johnnie Knox,
Foul fa their snash and scandal,
I hope in their confession box
Auld Nick pees on their candle.
They sair misca this haly man,
This foonder o oor nation,
And think nae ill this sanct to ban
For pride and fornication.

They aft repeat the country-clash
That lang syne at Lang Yester
When he was young he didna fash
The lassies a' to pester.
For they repeat and swear on aith
That yince when he was vogie
He fukkt a wife and dochter baith
Intil a wee killogie.

Noo I maintain this was nae sin,
Gin this be true, as may hap;
He rammed his argument weel in
And bridged the generation gap.
A man that had sic awesome pooer
That neither youth nor age could damp
And fukkt them baith in half an oor
Deserves his heid upon a stamp.

56

This wad be makin sma remeid
For sair neglect this mony a year,
Upon a stamp to pit his heid
Is less than justice done, I fear.
Na, let's be fair to Johnnie Knox
And to the man's abeelity;
Prent millions o guid upricht cocks
To honour his vireelity.

ROAD TO CARRINGTON

Along the road to Carrington
When lissom spring is here
The soft west wind shakes down in showers
The crabtree and the sloe-bush flowers,
The chaffinch rings his silver bell
From every hazel in the dell
And wayside whins are cushioned gold
Along the road to Carrington
Before the spring is old.

Along the road to Carrington
When summer fills the land
The dell's sea-green and shivering corn
Waves far along the blue-skied morn
And yonder where the hill-pines sway
The Moorfoot braes are swept all day
By wine-like winds from off the sea
Along the road to Carrington
By honey-scented lea.

Along the road to Carrington
When autumn gilds the green
The breeze that went to sleep at noon
Wakes up with twilight shades to croon
The twittering birds to rest where now
They perch on every sheltered bough,
While fields of stubble stretch afar
Along the road to Carrington
Beneath the evening star.

Along the road to Carrington
When winter comes at last
The furrows of the frosty field
Are filled with winter's death-white yield:
But such things are beyond our ken
For in some bielded but or ben
We sit, nor think that we should go
Along the road to Carrington
Amongst the drifting snow.

SNAWDON WOOD

The nicht we stood on Snawdon Hill,
Hoo mony winters syne,
When a' but yon snell win' was still
Three freits I ca' to min'.

Owerhead 'mang pines sae dowf wi snaw,
Deep in his mirkest derns,
The mune socht oot a waukrife craw;
He craiked to deive the sterns.

A houlet skraighed in Danskine Howe,
And through the flichteran snaw
We heard ootower the Rangely Knowe
The ghaist-bell o' Nunraw.

I gae nae mair forenent Bleak Law
Nor yet on Snawdon Hill,
But ower the grymin o' the snaw
Yon win' is soughan still.

And ay atween the mune and me
Cauld lies lown Lammermuir
Where rinnan ay and on I see
White winnle-wraiths o' stoor.

59

STARRY TALK

Venus in her best bri-nylon
Glides around the solar pylon
Heeding not that baleful cateran,
Sullen, leaden, distant Saturn
Linking at it in his sarc-
ophagus, a cosmic nark.

For I looked into the future
Far as human eye can see,
Saw the heavens filled with Pegasi
Of varying degree;
Millions of mus ridiculus
And elephants pediculous;
Each from his elevated station
Dispensed inspiring micturation.

Does elephantine ichor fall
Upon the Scots pragmatical?
'Tis just, for grave yet modest dews
Inspire stern Caledonia's muse,
And short, not very far between,
Are Pegasus' visits to the scene;
Like Halley's or like Encke's comet,
Or mid-slung coffin of Mahomet,
Once in every year or two
Scotland receives th' inspiring brew
And on poor mankind as a whole
Pours out at length her Doric soul,
While Earth, the nut, and Moon his sister,
In vain try ice-caps and a clyster;
Old Earth whom ne'er a globe surpasses
For poets, astronomers and asses.

60

THE STISHIE AT THE STEAMIE
(Jig Time: The Irish Washerwoman)

There was auld Mrs Mungo that wins at the bingo
And Mrs Nappollo that sells the ice-cream,
There was wee Mrs Rafferty, weedow MacCafferty,
Forbye Mrs Thin that's sae broad in the beam.
And naebody thocht that thon Wedensday moarnin
As they hurled their white things through Low'r Aibbeyhill
Whit a terrible stishie withoot ony warnin
Wad brak in a neebourhood peacefu and still.

There was forty or mair o that took to the flair o
The steamie they built near the auld picter-hoose;
As we got wir detergent we mindet the Regent
And the rerr nichts at Beggie baith canty and crouse.
Sune auld Miss Mackenzie and Jenny MacAlapin
Tummelt their sheets in the het reamin sowps
And syne wi their dollies they a' fell a-wallopin
Fower raws o sowdies a' waggin their dowps.

We mindet Kinneary, the cop they ca'd Fairy,
And puir weedow Kelly that lived on the dole,
A miner ca'ed Ritchie, his cock was ay itchy
The only bit clean when the rest was a' coal.
And hoo up at Baldy's we'd tanner fish-suppers
And skeechin in plenty a penny a gless,
Wi herrin and tatties and creeshy Fyne kippers
At fower for a tanner and torn-bellies less.

When it cam to aristos we beat a' the Bristos
The Happy Land tae and the Pleesance forbye,
We'd the Duke and the Yerl and Croon Princess Pearl
And the Duchess o Dumbiedykes that was ay dry.
Like auld Scotland's heroes, the Bruce and the Wallace,
The twae that stude up tae the hale English pooer,
They ay gaed in couples the Aibbeyhill polis
For fear they got tanked by some randy wee hure.

61

Noo it's wyce no to mention, or draw the attention
To Saughton, the Calton or e'en Peterheid,
Whaur his Majesty's pleesure got them muckle leesure,
Though the yins that was liftet are forty years deid.
But it chanct a grand-dochter o auld Michael Hammy
Wha was launched at Barlinnie frae aff the tap-deck
Saw glaiket May Black wi a cord o pajammy
For a joke mak a noose o't roond Jeannie Broon's neck.

She ups and she at her and stairtet to batter
Mey Black on the heid tae a'body's surprise,
For naeb'dy kent Hammy, nor heard o the rammy
In Glesgy whaur keelies get killed aff like flies.
Noo fat Mrs Thin she stude up for wee Blackie
And fetcht Mrs Hamilton yin on the gub;
We were shair that the stoun o't near garred her to cackie
And the wecht o the welt pit her intae the tub.

She cried for the mannie, "Tam Scott, my auld fanny
Is bubblin awa like a guid Irish stew."
He dialled for emergency, fire, and detergency,
"Nine-ninety-nine" as weel's "One-two, one-two."
Sune doon the Canigate sirens were wailin,
Fower amblances cam and sax fire-engines too,
Twal struck frae the Aibbey, the schules were a' skailin,
There was crowds frae the boozers and some frae the broo.

Mrs Thin was arrestit because she'd molestit
And Hammy was up for disturbance o peace.
The wordy auld Beylie, fat Jonathan Riley,
Says, "It's really disgraceful that City Police,
Loyal men and trustworthy fine upstanding ossifers
Should be called from their duties and fire-engines too,
And men like myself, wise and witty philosophers,
Must waste precious time on such wretches as you."

"Mrs Hemilton, Em'ly, a good Scottish fem'ly,
You say you were tot'ly immersed in the tubs?"
"Aye, up to the shouthers in het washin' pouthers,
My fanny, my belly and even my bubs."
Noo, this shockin admission was never reportit
And you'd never hae heard o the stishie at a'
(For by Press and by Polis the thing was distortit)
But for me there disguised as a Flee on the Wa'.

62

TWAL OORS IN PARADISE

The Lord's taen up twal stane o stour
To mak a man within the oor;
He filled it neist wi bluid and sweit
And stude the cratur on its feet;
"For twa oors noo gie nomenclature
Tae a' the bestiary o nature!"
Then God gied him an oor's sedation,
Cut oot his rib for Eve's creation;
When he awoke the simple eediot
Fell deep in love and wed immediate;
For three oors without kirk or papers
They cut some matrimonial capers,
Though Eve foond time 'twixt copulations
To share wi Satan fruit collations;
Wi knowledge o the guid and evil
She glaikt puir Adam to the Deevil,
And or the nock had chappit twice
God pit them oot o Paradise.

WHITEST PEBBLE ON SANNA'S SHORE

I found my true love in Ardnamurchan,
The whitest pebble on Sanna's shore;
O, there I met her and there I lost her;
It grieves my heart for evermore.

I sought great glory with royal Chairlie
And found yon dreary Drummossie Moor;
In dark and secret homeward turning
I met my love on Sanna's shore.

O, brief and tearful our life-long parting
To follow Chairlie across the main;
My whitest pebble beyond the tangle,
My love alone in wind and rain.

Pale moon arising o'er Ardnamurchan,
O, cruel ship's wake that cleft the sea;
In dreams alone now I see my true love
Who stands for ay awaiting me.

I found my true love in Ardnamurchan
The whitest pebble on Sanna's shore;
O, there I met her and there I lost her;
It grieves my heart for evermore.

GLOSSARY OF SCOTS, Etc.

The meanings are applicable to poems in this book.
In some instances no adequate English expression exists.
The Scots I use is mainly a spoken language so the spelling, being phonetic, varies.

A.

a'	all
aboon	above
ac'	act
accoutrit	decked out
ae	single one
a-fitterin	tampering
aiblins	perhaps
aik	oak
aiker	shadowy flicker
ain	own
aince	once
airms	arms
airn	iron
aith	oath
ane-and-thrie	one-and-three (6p)
antran	occasional
assize	trial, court of justice
athort	athwart
atweel	indeed
atween	between
auld	old
awa	away
ay	for ever

B.

baccies	tobaccos
bailie	magistrate
baith	both
ballant	ballad
ballop	trouser-fly
bandy	bow-legged

65

banes	bones
baney	bony
barley-brie	whisky
barry	wheel-barrow
baukin	spectre, bogey
baund	band (music)
beek	bask
begood	began
belly-thraw	indigestible food
ben	inside room
beylie	bailie, magistrate
bieldy	sheltered
bigg, big	build
bink	bees' nest
bird-thrang	filled with birds
birl	whisk round
birsled	bristled, roasted
blae	blue
blaeberries	blueberries
blaired	bleached by sun and wind
blate	shy
bleerit	bleary
blether	stammer
blinner	blinder
blitter	snipe
bloody-bells	fox-gloves
blythe	merry
bock	retch
bodies	persons
booer	bower
boozers	public-houses, drunkards
bosky	woody
bouksome	swollen-bellied
bourach	confused heap
bourtree	elder-tree
braes	hill-slopes
braikens, breckan	bracken
brak	break
brammles	brambles
braw	of fine appearance
bree, brie	brew, broth
brie	brow
breenged	rushed violently
breid	bread

66

brek	break
brocht to bairn	heavy with child
broo	brew
broo	brow
broo	labour bureau (Dept. of Social Security)
brook	enjoy the use of
bruiket	spoilt, dirtied
brunt-oot	burnt out
buik-chapman	book salesman
buiks	books
bund	bound
bykefu	nest full of bees

C.

cackie	excrement
cailliach, caillie	old woman, hag
caird	tinker
callant	boy
cam	came
camsteerie	perverse, cross-grained
cannle	candle
cannle-dowp	candle-stump
canty	merry, contented
carlin	witch, old woman
cast	cast-iron
cat-loup	a short distance
cauld	cold
causey	paving-stone
cervine-heid	head like a deer
chalder	large Scots dry measure= 8 quarters
chappin, chappit	(clock) striking, struck
chaumer	chamber-pot
chiel	fellow
chimley	chimney
chirmed	warbled on a low note
chows	chews
Chreest	an oath (Gaelic pronunciation)
chuckie, chuckie stane	pebble
clairty	filthy
clappin	caressing, petting

67

clart	dirt
cleed, cled	to clothe, clad
clegs	horse-flies
clotched	messed about
collieshangie	rough-house
cooerin	cowering
cope	sell
country-clash	rural gossip
covins, covens	witches' sabbaths
cowp, cowpit	upset, decant
crabbie	ill-natured
crack	conversation
craigs	necks
craik	croak
cramosie	crimson stuff (velvet)
crampet	confined
crannie	small finger, thin twig
cratur	creature
creesh	grease
crom	bent
croon	crown
crouse	lively, comfortable
crowdie	gruel, sour milk, cheese
cuddies	horses, donkeys
cuist	cast
cuitrin	coaxing
curmurrin	rumbling in guts

D.

dang	struck
dashielaggie	colt's-foot, or tussilago farfara
dauch, davoch	(Scots) large area of arable (416 acres)
dauchy	sloppy
daw	dawn
deemas	considerable
deil	devil
deived	deafened
dern	secret
deuks	ducks
dicht	wipe
dinger	heavy stroke
dirled	tingled, rattled
div	do

dochter	daughter
dockans	dock-plants
doited	crazy with age
dominus	master
dookit	ducked
doon	down
doon-borne	oppressed, near child-labour
doot	doubt
dour	stubborn, sullen
dowf	sad
dowie	dismal
dowp	backside
dozen	quieten down
drappit	dropped
dree his weird	endure his fate
dreep	drop, strain (potatoes)
dreich, dreichsome	dreary
dreids	dreads
drooled	drivelled
drooned	drowned
droukt	soaked
drouthy	thirsty
drow	heavy dew
drucken	drunken
dry-dyke	dry-stone wall, unmortared
dugs	dogs

E.

edders	adders
ee-banes	eye-holes in skull
e'er	ever
eild	old age
eird	earth
eird-fast	earth-bound
elder	Presbyterian church office-holder
endite	to record
erse, ersehole	arse, arsehole
erse-for-elbae	tightly packed crowd
ettle	to try
exorceese	exorcise (evil spirits)
extempore	instantaneously

F.

fain	eager
fankled	entangled
fanny	woman's pudendum
farls	thick oatcakes
fash	trouble
fause	false
feak-rock	sedimentary rock, lime or sand-stone
feerdie	sturdy
fell	extremely
ferlie	unnatural, wonderful sight
fersellin	fermenting
fient a—	nothing, damn all
fieres	companions
flair	floor
flannen	flannel
flaughterer	peat or turf cutter
fley	frighten
flicher	flicker
flicht	flight
flichter	fickle flight (as of snowflakes)
flude	flood
foggy-bumbees	wild, bumble-bees
foonds	foundations
forbye	as well
forefend	prevent
foreknew	prophesied
forenent	opposite
forfochtan	exhausted
forpit	Edinburgh dry measure, $\frac{1}{8}$ or $\frac{1}{4}$ stone
foul fa	a curse on—
fower	four
fowth	abundance
freits	unnatural sights
frustra	frustration
fu	full, drunk
fushionless	pithless
furthy	frank
futtret	weasel

70

G.

gadged	gauged
gae, gaed	go, went
gairds	guards
gairters	garters
gaither	gather
galore	plenty
gang	go
gangrel	tramp, vagabond
gansel	harsh garlic sauce
gantin	gaping stupidly
gar	make or force, compel
gargrugous	austere
gash	grim, ghastly
gashled	distorted
gerss	grass
geyan, gey	very, extremely
ghaist	ghost
gin	if
glaikit	simple-minded
glunch	look morosely
goonie	night-dress
goved	stared
gowk	fool, cuckoo
gravats	scarves
greetit	wept
grew	intense shivering
grool	gruel, mush
grun	ground
grushy	flabby
grymin	sprinkling
gub	mouth
guid-faith	mild oath, good faith!
guid-gaun	progressing steadily
guid-will	goodwill
gull	low growl
gundy-gutted	pot-bellied
gurly	uneven, rough-surfaced
gutsy	greedy

71

H.

haar	coastal fog
hae	have
Hagh!	call of long-eared owl
hain	guard, protect
hainberry	raspberry
hairm	harm
hairst	harvest
hallion	kitchen-boy, scullion
hamehald	territory
hame-seik	homesick
hansel	handsel, have a first taste of
happit	wrapped
haud, hauden	hold, held
haud forth	harangue
hauf	half
hauf-croon	half-a-crown (12½p)
haugh	river-meadow
haughed	guttural cry of long-eared owl
hawkit	chapped, red-raw skin
hawkit	exposed for sale, whored
heezed	hoisted
heids	heads
herberie	harborage, safe haven
herdit	shepherded
hert	heart
hert-eident	constant, enduring
het	hot
hiddy-giddy	turmoil
hie	high
hing	hang
hingy	overcast, showery
hizzy	hussy
hoo	how
hoodies, hoodie-craws	carrion crows
hooed	hooted
hoose-end	gable
horn	sexual desire
houlet	owl
howe-dumb-deid	midnight
howff	resort, tavern

72

howk	delve
hugger-mugger	in confusion
hur, hure	whore
hurled	wheeled

I.

ilk	each
intil	within

J.

jeckets	jackets
jeests	joists
john	penis

K.

kain	rent, in kind
keckles	cackles
ked	sheep-tick
keekit	peeped
keelies	roughs
Keevit!	cry of long-eared owl
keigh	ordure
keisty	lecherous
kenna	know not
kenned	known
killogie	floor-space before a kiln
kiltet	kilted
kinna	kind of
kirn	churn
kirstened	christened
kittle	tickle
krecked	croaked
kye	cattle
kytes	bellies
kythe	wishing to be friendly

L.

lade	mill-stream
laigh	low
lang	long
lang-luggit-houlet	long-eared owl
lantron	lantern
lauch, leuch	to laugh, a laugh
lee-lang	live-long
leid	language, bird song
leid	lead (metal)
liftet	arrested
limmer	rascal
lintie	brown linnet
lippen	confidently trust
loanin	country lane
lowe	glow
lown	peaceful, calm
lowp, loup	jump
lowse	loosen, set free
ludgers	lodgers
lugs	ears
lume	tool, penis
lunts	draws at a pipe of tobacco
lustra	period of five years

M.

mair	more
makar	poet
mappamoond	map of the earth
mavis	song-thrush
mauchy	dirty, repulsive
maun	must
mawk, mawkie	maggot
melled	mixed
mergh	marrow
merle	blackbird
Mey	May (month, or woman's name)
micht	might (subjunctive)
milsey	milk-strainer
min'	mind

74

mindet	remembered
mint, ment	threaten
mirk, mirkest	dark, darkest
misca	miscall
mislairt	mistaken
mither	mother
moo	mouth
mowe	fuck
muckle	great
muir-spade	peat-spade
mune	moon
mutchkin	pint-pot
mysel	myself

N.

narr	growl
neb	nose,beak
neebour	neighbour
neesy	snorting
neist	next
neives	fists
nicht	night
nicht-couls	night-caps
nisi dominus frustra	motto of Edinburgh, "In vain without God"
no	not
nock	clock
noo	now

O.

ondeemas	incalculable
oor	hour
oor	our
ootower	over the top of
oot-through	through the middle of
or	before, ere
ower-true	unluckily indisputable

P.

pang-fu	chock-full, crammed
pannicle	short transparent skirt
parritch	porridge
partan	edible crab

75

pat	pot
pauchles	beggars
pauchly	beggarly
paul	puzzle
peat-bree	stagnant peat-pools
peat-coom	peat-dust
peep-hole	beadle's spy-hole in church-door
peeries	spinning-tops
pen'	pend, alleyway
pentit	painted
pey	pay
philapeg	kilt
pield	bald
pillions	tatters
pingles	small cooking-pots
pit	put
pith	strength
ploiter	wade about in mud, etc.
polis	police
poolies	head-lice
pouks	pucks, sprites, Will o' wisps
pouthers	powders
powes	heads
pownie	pony
prent	print
puddock	frog
puir-moothed	pulling a discontented face
pu'pit	pulpit
pynour	pioneer, the queen wasp seeking stuff for nest.

Q.

quaich	shallow drinking-cup
quarneld-broo	square-faced

R.

rairs	roars
raivel	tangle
rammies	tumults
randy	hot-tempered, termagant
rapt	raped
raw	row
rax	reach
rax a dinger	strike a hard blow

reams, reamin	flows frothily
reek, reekt	smoke, smoked
reestit	smoke-dried
reid	red
rerr	rare, delicious, exciting
rigbane	backbone
rime	hoar-frost
rosetty	resinous
rowth, routh	plenty
rowts	bellows, roars
ruggit	tore at
ruttin	(stag) in heat

S.

sabbin-sauch	weeping-willow
sae	so
sair	grievous, painful
sanct, sanctly	saint, saintly
sandy-mills	sand-castles
sate	sat
sauch	willow
saul	soul
saut	salt
sawins	sawdust
scabbit	scabby
scairtin	scratching
schule	school
sclim	climb
screes	detritus, stony slopes
scunner, scunnersome	violent distaste, and what induces it
ser, sert	serve, served
serk	shirt
sermon-gless	preacher's hour-glass
shair	sure
shanks	legs
shanty	chamber-pot
sharn	dung
shaw	small wood, or flat valley
shaw	to show
shoogled	shook violently to and fro
shouthers	shoulders

shusy	chassis, corpse
sic, siccan	such
sich	sigh
sicht	sight
simmer	summer
sin	since
skail	spill
skarnochin	tumultuous storm
skeechin	ale made with treacle
skellied-een	cross-eyed
skink	bad meat
skirl	screech
skitter	diarrhoea
sklent	to cast obliquely
skraighs	shrieks
slaver	slobber, drivel
slorach	ropy slime
slorp	to swallow noisily
smoorit	smothered
snash	ill-natured speech
snaw	snow
snaw-bree	ice-cold water
sneeshit	sneezed
snell	bitterly cold
socht	sought
sodgers	soldiers
soo	sow
soor	sour
soss	badly cooked mess
souch, souchin	deep sigh
sowdies	slovenly women
sowps	soap-suds
spangs	leaps violently out
speetit	spitted
speir	ask
speldered	outstretched
splairge	splash
splore	spree
spunge	putrid moisture
stachert	staggered
staive	heavy blow
stane	stone
stanel	kestrel
stang-aither	adder

stark-deid	stone-dead
stauns	stands
steamie	public washhouse, laundry
steeks	stitches
steered, steerin	disturbed, boisterous
stent	allotted task
sterns	stars
stippet	stupid
stishie	uproar
stot	bull, clumsy fellow
stoun	shock with a blow
stour	dust
strae	straw
stramash	uproar
strath	wide valley
stroan	urinate copiously, pour out
stude	stood
stuffy	substantial, enduring
sucker	sugar
swats	new ale
sweir	unwilling
sweit	sweat
swither	hesitate
syne	since, the past

T.

taen	taken
taen up wi	pleased with
taet	tiny amount, lump (of sugar)
taid	toad
tanked	violently assaulted
tatties	potatoes
terse	pudendum
teuch	tough
the-year	this present year
thir	these
thirteen-pointer	stag with thirteen pointed antlers
thocht	thought
tholed	endured
thon	yon
thrang	busy, crowded
thrashes	bull-rushes

thretty-seiven	thirty-seven
thrissles	thistles
thunnerin	thundering
thunnerspate	violent thunderstorm
thurible	censer
timmer	timber
tine	to lose
tirl	rasp at the door knocker
tither	the other
toon	town
torn-bellies	kippered herring torn in curing
touch	rotten wood
tramort	corpse
trinklin	tinkling
tuim	empty
tummelt	tumbled
twa, twae	two
twal	twelve
twalmonth	full year
twatt	penis, pudendum
tykes	dogs

U.

ultra vires	beyond your power (legal term)
unbruikt	virgin, unspoilt
unhained	boundless
unhyne	immensely evil
unkirstened	unchristened

V.

vaunty	boastful
vogie	sexually excited

W.

waar	broken stuff, rubbish
wabbit	weak, spindly
wad	would
wadger	wager
waesome	sad

80

waggitty	pendulum wall-clock
waif	paltry, very frail
waitter-bailie	water-, river-bailiff
waled	selected
wallop	to rush clumsily
walth	wealth
wambles	rumbles in belly
wame	belly
wauchle	wagging
waukrife	wide awake, unable to sleep
waur	worse
weans	children
wear	to move gradually
wedders	male sheep
wee	small
weedowed	widowed
weel-biled	well-boiled
weicht	weight
weird	fate
weirdie	smallest bird of a hatching
welt	seam of a shoe
welt	pudendum
wesp	wasp
wey	way
whatna	what kind of?
whaur	where
wheech	sudden movement, stink of flatus
wheen	a few, uncertain number
wheenged	whimpered
whinger	cutlass
whins	gorse, furze
whit	what
white things	white cotton or linen washing
whudder	heavy rushing sound
whuff	whiff, pinch (of snuff)
whurry	scratch or whizz off
wid	wood, thicket
win in, win to	attain to, reach
winnle-wraith	spectre raised by the wind, mirage
wir	our
wittrous	very bad-tempered
wizened	withered, dried up
wonnert	wondered
wot, wat	got to know

81

wran	wren
wrocht	fashioned, wrought
wrunkled	wrinkled
wud	mad
wyce	sensible, wise
wytes	responsibilities

Y.

yairds	yards (36 ins.)
yeld	barren
yett	gate
yeukie	itchy
yill	ale
yin	one
yird	earth, piece of ground
yird-blast	violent gust rising off ground
yoke on	attack, assault
yollerin	confused bellowing
yont	beyond
yowes	ewes

GLOSSARY OF PROPER NAMES

A

Aibbeyhill	Abbeyhill, suburb of East Edinburgh, near Holyrood Palace.
Albert's widdy	Queen Victoria after 1861, when Prince Albert died.
Anstruther Wester	Ancient parish of East Fife.

B

Baldy's	A well-known fish and chip emporium.
Barlinnie	Prison in Glasgow.
Beggie	Dr. Begg's Buildings, Abbeyhill, now demolished.
Belchie (Aillie)	Alison Bellsches, a farm-worker.
Beltane Day	May Day or Midsummer festival.
Ben More	Name of several hills, all prominent.
Berwick's Boond	The Bounds of Berwick, separating it from Scotland.
Billie	An ancient Berwickshire parish.
Billiemire	An extensive bog in above, now reclaimed.
Bite-aboot	A farm near Duns.
Black Friday	Name of any disastrous Friday: here a fishing disaster.
Blackhope Scar	The highest hill in the Moorfoots, marked by deep ravines.
Blanerne	A farm and castle-site near Duns.
Blaweary	Common name for a bleak area.
Bleak Law	A foothill of the Lammermoors.
Bowdler (Rev. Thos.)	The well-known purger of Shakespeare and Gibbon.
Bristos	Various streets in a suburb of S. Edinburgh.
Bull (John, eediot)	A figure for England, referring to the idiot heir to Duke of Queensberry who roasted a kitchen boy (Scotland).
Bunkle	Part of a united Berwickshire parish.

C

Calton	The Calton Jail formerly on Calton Hill, Edinburgh.
Canogate, Canigate	The ancient burgh of the Canongate near old Edinburgh.

83

Carlin's Loups	Carlops, a village in the Pentland Hills.
Carnethie	A prominent hill in the Pentlands.
Carrington	An ancient Midlothian village.
Carron	Ironworks near Carron, Stirlingshire.
Carter Fell	High hill in the Cheviots.
Cassandra.	A prophetess; also the name of Ronsard's lady-love.
Catraeth	Ancient battle between Britons and Anglo-Saxons.
Catrail	Mysterious turf-wall built as a tribal boundary in Scottish borders.
Chirnside	A Berwickshire village.
Christ's Kirk at the Tron	The old name of the Tron Church, Edinburgh, scene of former Hogmonay assemblies.
Cloich	Hills in Peeblesshire.
Co'burn Law	A prominent hill in Berwickshire, Cockburn Law.
Corvus Corone	Latin name of the carrion crow.
Coul MacFinn	A generic name for any big-hearted Irishman (cf. Finn MacCoul).
Craig Taw	A rock-stack near St. Abb's head.
Croon Princess	A pun. A whore who charged a crown! (25p).
Cymri	The comrades. The ancient Welsh in adversity.

D

Danskin Howe	Valley of the Danskine (Denmark) Burn, East Lothian.
Dindreich	"Hill of the Bluff", in the West Moorfoots.
Dineiddyn	Dunedin, ancient town of the British Gododdin tribe, near Edinburgh.
Doolaw	A hill near St. Abb's head; also a farm.
Doric	Pertaining to Northern Greece, or Scotland.
Droedan	A Berwickshire bogey-man.
Duchess o Dumbiedykes	A notorious inhabitant of central Edinburgh suburb.
Duke	A pretentious fellow in East Edinburgh.
Dunse	Duns, birthplace of John Duns Scotus, famous mediaeval schoolman.

Dutch leid	Refers to equestrian statue of Chas. II in Edinburgh, cast in lead by Dutch sculptor.
Dye	A small stream in Lammermoors.

E

Eird	The Earth.
Embro	Edinburgh.
Encke's Comet	A comet, of period 3.3 years, named after Encke, German astronomer.
Erse	Irish Gaelic language.
Esk	Midlothian river.
Eye	Small Berwickshire stream.

F

Fairy	Policeman named after P.C. Fairyfeet, in "Comic Cuts".
Falkirk	Scottish town with well-known ice-rink.
Fanna Hill	A prominent but little-known Border hill.
Ford	Midlothian village on the Tyne.
Forest	Ettrick Forest, a large Border region, no longer well-wooded (Selkirkshire).
Flatterstane	Flotterstone, a hamlet near the Pentland Hills.
Frisian	Germanic invaders of coastal Britain.
Fyne	Loch Fyne, famed for herrings.

G

Gabriel's Trump	The trump of Doomsday.
Gala	Tributary of Tweed, draining Moorfoot Hills.
Gibbon (Edward)	The historian author of "Decline and Fall of the Roman Empire," expurgated by Bowdler.
Glen Leevit	Gaelic pronunciation of Glen Livet (whisky).
Gododdin	Ancient British tribe of N.E. coast cf. Votadini.
Gogledd	Old Welsh name of S.E. Scotland "The Lost North" anciently their Kingdom.

Gowfers' Land	A tenement off the Canongate where golfers met. "Eheu fugaces! 'Alas the flights" refers to golf and time.
Gwenhwyfar	Welsh name of Arthur's queen.
Gwynion	Welsh name of Castle Guinnion scene of Arthur's 8th battle.

H

Halley's Comet	Prominent comet which caused alarm early last century.
Happy Land	An ironic name for a sleazy area of Edinburgh.
Hawick	Border town famous for rugby and mills
Hawthornden	Site of the poet Drummond's residence on the Esk, Midlothian.
Heriot	Ancient parish in Moorfoot Hills.
Hogmonay, Hogmanay	New Year's Eve famed for traditional customs.
Hopes	Valleys, suitable for rearing sheep.
Hume Tooer	A prominent ruin on the Lammermuir foothills.
Hurker	A rock-stack near St. Abb's Head.

J

Jag	A pun. Jaguar motor-car or prick from thorn.
Janus	The two-faced classical figure. The Tolbooth clock in the Canongate has two faces.
Jezebels	A figure for loose women.

K

Kelsae	Kelso, border town on the confluence of Tweed and Teviot.
Kelvinside	A stylish residential area of Glasgow.
King's Park	A superior suburb of Glasgow.
Kittlenakit	Derivation obscure, ancient place-name of several Scottish hamlets.
Knox (John)	Joannes Cnoxus, the reformer.
Kyles o Bute	Picturesque part of Firth of Clyde, near Rothesay.

L

Lammas	Early August; ancient feast-day.
Lammer	The hill district of S.E. Scotland.
Lammermoor	Same as above.

86

Lang Yester	A hamlet in upper East Lothian.
Larmor	Physicist associated with Lorentz.
Lauderdale	A district of Berwickshire, valley of R. Leader.
Lawheid Hill	A small prominence in Pentlands, where the Covenanters camped prior to the battle, Nov. 28, 1666.
Leigate Lade	A pond or channel where Aillie Belchie drowned her children.
Leith	Ancient seaport, rival of Edinburgh, now abandoned.
Lintlaw Haugh	A small valley near Chirnside.
Loch Katrine	Romantic beauty spot in Trossachs, Glasgow's water supply.
Logan's Crag	A picturesque precipice with waterfall, Pentland Hills.
Longbottom	Mythical subject of comic epitaph. "Here lies John Longbottom aged 20 years, artist: Ars longa, vita brevis."
Lorentz	Dutch physicist concerned with pre-Einstein problems.
Loth	Ancient name of traditional King of Lothian.
Lowden.	Lothian.
Lowdenburn	Stream marking Edinburgh-Midlothian boundary.

M

MacCallein More	A title of the Duke of Argyll.
MacDiarmid	Hugh MacDiarmid, illustrious Scottish poet.
Mah Jong	Ancient Chinese table game; taken up in the West in this century.
Mahoun	Medieval Scots name for Mahomet. Anti-Christ, the Devil.
Marie	Marie Stuart, Queen of Scots.
Medraut	Arthur's bastard who rebelled against him.
Meg	Margaret, the lady on Edinburgh's coat-of-arms.
Midside Maggie	A famous Berwickshire worthy, of Lauderdale.
Montrose (Marquis)	James Graham, executed in Edinburgh 1650.

87

Moorfoots	A range of hills in Northern part of Southern Uplands of Scotland (properly Mur-Thwaite=moor-stretch).
Moray House	Ancient town house in Edinburgh.
Morley	Physicist who conducted experiments on speed of light.
Myrddin	The Welsh name of Merlin, a British prince driven mad by the slaughter at the battle of Ardyrdd.

N

Norman-French	A bastard tongue spoken in Scotland and England after the Conquest.
Nunraw	A nunnery of the Cistercian order in East Lothian, near Gifford.

O

Owain	A Welsh prince slain in battle in 6th century. Son of King Urien of Wreged. His elegy was sung by the poet Taliesin.

P

Peel Fell	Prominent hill in middle Cheviots.
Pegasos, Pegasus	Greek winged horse, inspirer of poets.
Penmanshiel	A farm in Berwickshire.
Peterheid	Jail in Aberdeenshire.
Pishwanton	A wood and ancient hamlet near Lammermoors.
Playhoose Close	Alleyway off Canongate where anciently a theatre aroused tumults.
Pleesance	The Pleasance, anciently a country lane, latterly a slum.
Polwart	Polwarth, Berwickshire village.
Puddock-hole	Any wretched hamlet.

Q

Queensberry's Ha	The town house of the Dukes of Queensberry, off the Canongate.

R

Rammel	A wild bay filled with wreckage near St. Abb's Head.
Rangely Knowe	A small hill in the Lammermoors.
Ravenburn	A ruined cottage and stream in upper Jed valley (Cheviots).
Reel o' Tulloch	A Highland dance.

88

Regent	A disused picture-house in East Edinburgh.
Rullion Green	An upland hollow in Pentlands, scene of battle in 1666.

S

St. Paul	City on Mississippi in Minnesota.
Sandy's Sheuch	Hell, Sheuch being a deep gully and Sandy the Devil.
Saughton	Jail in Edinburgh.
Selkirk	Border town on the Ettrick.
Sharon	A pun. A region of Palestine; cow-dung (Scots).
Slaver Nick	The Devil. Queensberry house was as tall as a galleon.
Snawdon Wood	Snawdon, a farm and district near the Lammermoor.
Sodger's Law	A hill overlooking the sea near St. Abb's Head.
Strathclyde	Old Kingdom of Britons; modern region of Scotland.
Strix Otus	Latin name of long-eared owl.
Swithin (Saint)	Anglo-Saxon Saint who allegedly objected to being reburied, and caused forty days downpour.

T

Timnath	Philistine town where Samson got his wife.
Tinkler Mey	A border virago.
Tolbooth, To'boo	The jail and burgh-house of the Canongate.
Twiggies	A pun. Twigs and lanky ladies of pleasure.
Tynninghame	Ancient Anglian village near mouth of Lothian Tyne.

U

Unco Guid	The pious; whited sepulchres.

W

Warld's End Close	An alleyway in the Canongate where millennial doom-watchers met.
Weir, (Ketrail) Major	The wizard, burnt with his magic staff at Greenside, near Edinburgh.

89

Weir's Close	Alleyway named after another citizen named Weir.
White Horse Close	A courtyard at the bottom of the South-back Canongate. Edinburgh terminus of the London coach.
Wilson (Mt.)	High mountain in U.S.A. on which is an observatory.
Wodin	Norse hero who warred with the Jotuns.

Y

Yarrow	Tributary of the Tweed, scene of many ballads and songs.
Yerl	Earl, presumptuous scallywag of Old Edinburgh.

NOTES ON POEMS

Not every poem in this book is self-explanatory, though I should hope every one conveys something: for I have in many cases laboured to be plain and to keep as close as possible to the natural flow of speech, either in Scots or English; some rustic pieces, being a true mirror to observable nature, required little manipulation. Still, I hope the reader will find a few lines about the context of some poems will add to the interest.

AILLIE BELCHIE

In Dr. George Henderson's "Sayings of Berwickshire" (Newcastle 1856), under the heading "Sinned to the Nineteenth Degree", we read of the unfortunate Aillie Belchie, or Alison Bellsches on whose fate I founded this ballad. Like Tess of the D'Urbervilles, Aillie was of noble descent, from the crusading Norman family De Bellassize. Her tragic destiny was, no doubt, brought about by the unrestrained instincts which were her sole inheritance. She was harshly judged in her narrow environment of time and place. My last verse suggests that in the end she may have been forgiven.

BEN BOWDER

In 1975, thinking that the sesquicentenary of Bowdler's death in 1825 should be noted in appropriate form I sent this bit of bowdlerised baladinage to the Times Lit. Supp. The editor sent me word that he was hesitant about printing it and decided not to; so the opportunity to the literary establishment of doing Bowdler some sort of justice was lost, but for its inclusion here.

BIRD-SANG IN STRATHCLYDE

This, a philological study, will be obnoxious to owlish philologists who cannot stand facetiousness. Nevertheless I give examples of four strata of languages to be found in any Strathclyde quarry. Lowest in time is Old Wallensian, or Welsh, in which mad Merlin, in the embodiment of a cuckoo, still goes about saying, "Cw, cw, myn ghu?" (Where, where, my doggie?"), myn ghu or Mungo being the pet-name of St. Kentigern, Glasgow's patron saint. Other tongues co-exist uneasily today. They are broad Westland Scots, a species of acquired English, and Glaswegian. My line, "Ilk ane keeps its ain leid" refers to the original meaning of leid, as bird-song (leden in Old English and lieder in German), not language, generally.

BLACK FRIDAY

The Eyemouth disaster, October 1881, was caused by a sudden storm from the North-east which threw up the herring fishers' bodies around their own harbour. Half the town was widowed, included the grandmother of a friend of mine, Dick Macfarlane.

91

CLARTY KIRSTAN

Another earthy fruit from the unique Henderson orchard in Berwickshire. I have not done Kirstan's clartiness full justice as I wished to emphasise the funny side of it. Dr. Henderson called Kirstan "a complete earthworm". But, as I have written for her epitaph, versifying Dr. Henderson's "She is gone where the dirty and the clean are all on the same level".

> She is gane, she is gane
> Where the gerss is evergreen,
> And there's nae distinction drawn
> Betwixt the clarty and the clean.

CYMRIC FASTNESS

This fortress of the ancient Strathclyde Welsh is Hodge Cairn above Gala Water, which I have identified with Castle Guinnion, or the Fort of the White People where, traditionally, Arthur fought the eighth of his twelve battles. At Guinnion he twice in one day defeated two separate armies of Anglian invaders.

As in all Welsh poems of the cywydd form, the poet stands in a wilderness and conducts a conversation with natural objects, the theme being often a sad reflection on the glories of the past ages. Symbolically, night is falling, and the moon, coloured copper, mocks the golden face of the setting sun. The ghosts of the ancient Cymri reappear in the form of birds, of flowers, of of fruits indigenous to the slopes of Castle Guinnion, which by its hilly nature and because of the massive stones of the ancient broch, fallen into a cairn, has never known the plough, and is therefore, according to the troubadours, a place under Arthur's protection.

DYING TESTAMENT OF A VICTORIAN PHYSICIST

Old beliefs die hard. In 1934, when I wrote this satire, the Special Theory of Relativity was exercising some people; me, in a small naive way, among them.

ERSEHOLE O' CREATION

Burns, in his first Border Tour, in 1787, did not much admire the bleak grandeur of the Lammermuir and described it in a telling phrase, applied to poor land in Ayrshire and elsewhere. Long ago, I often crossed the same area on foot in midwinter as well as in other seasons following Burns' footsteps, or rather his horse's. I should rather have described the desolation as "the backside of the moon," with which phrase a shepherd friend agreed.

FOUR GATES OF LOTHIAN

Inspired by a verse from Revelations. This poem appeared, in the amateur "Border Magazine," printed by Mr. Sanderson in Peebles, 1928. It so impressed Albert Mackie that it was one of a very few he brought back from Glasgow in 1946 when he became editor of the "Edinburgh Evening Dispatch" and set about printing (and paying for) local poets' work preparatory to the inauguration of the Festival. This gnomic poem was one of the first printed, and paid for, like the others.

HE WINNA DAE FOR ME

As William Dunbar tells us, even kings of old Scotland were practical in love-affairs and if we read "In Secret Place" or "The Wowing of the King quhen he wes in Dunfermling" we find that the gentle maidens were not so naive either in affairs of the heart, or whatever organ is the seat of Venus.

HERBERIE

A true description of my cottage on Heriot Water where I prefer to live in the style of previous centuries. The cottage is of great age which can be proved by a line of a local ballad of places in the parish;

"In Sunnyside a wabster guid."

In the beginning of the 19th century there was an entire "toun" of weavers on the hill half-a-mile distant, who migrated to Galashiels at that time. So the "wabsters" of Sunnyside must have flourished very long before 1800. William Dunbar, in the "Lament for the Makars" mentions "Heryot" as a deceased poet, probably the Rector of the parish at the end of the 15th century. But nothing has been known of him or his poems since death "hes tane (him) out of this cuntre". He probably visited Sunnyside in his parish duties. No work of Heryot has survived.

HOGMANAY

In this phantasmagoria I transcend time and space in my Hogmanay stagger up the chief thoroughfare of my native town where I once could tell, on a dark night, by the smell, which close I was passing.

I was also acquainted in my boyhood with much of the tradition of the Canongate and High Street. It is not possible, in the short space of a note to explain my many references to tradition, from White Horse Close to the Tron. The persevering inquirer would be well advised to read Chambers' "Traditions of Edinburgh" or Grant's "Old and New Edinburgh". The Norman-French means, "Help, English! The worse for you if he gets me with child".

KITTLENAKIT HOP

Rubens' "La Kermesse" depicts an open-air harvest thanksgiving with all the gusto of Flemish peasant life. "Kittlenakit Hop" is a Scottish version of this, set in a winter scene such as Breughel might have delineated. Obviously this is written from personal observation.

There are several places called Kittlenakit in Scotland; in Fife, and Angus, as well in the Lammermuirs. Here is a local rhyme, containing some of the Berwickshire place-names in my ballad:

Lochirmacus, Dunse and Langton,
Pouterlynie and Pishwanton,
Kittlenakit and Cornysyke,
In Elfhole is the Devil's byke.

LOWDEN LASS

My first attempt at Scots verse, based on my Pentland wanderings. The speaker is a Covenanter, exiled after Bothwell Brig. Albert Mackie and I were alike in our early attachment to the "Hills of Home".

93

MACLEAN THE CIRCUS POWNIE

The Dutch original by Edmond de Clercq was written half-a-century ago but I could get no information from Meulenhoff, the publishers of this poem, about Clercq. The poem, apart from its sympathetic note, was also so akin in vocabulary to Scots that I could not resist turning it into my mother tongue.

The first couplet compelled me:

Op aard is niets zo droef misschien
als het kleine circuspaard MacLean.

ON CEMENTING LEVEL THE STABLE FLOOR, Etc.

This epigrammatic summary of the status of man, in relation to brute, came upon me instantaneously in the stable of the manse where James Macdonald, that ill-fated genius, friend of Goethe, Lessing, etc. spent five tempestuous years before going to his destruction in Europe on a chivalrous adventure. I did not know of Macdonald when I wrote the verses, and years later it struck me that I was describing his very feelings when he condemned the narrowness of the Fife clergy of his time. "A Hebridean in Goethe's Weimar" (Blackwell) gives Macdonald's story.

PHALLATELY FOR JOHNNY KNOX

A strong lobbying for his representation on a stamp in 1972, the quater-centenary of Knox's death, by Scottish philatelists and others, was ignored by the P.M.G. who gave a sop in the form of an emasculated Knox print on envelopes. Knox is still a controversial figure, an enfant terrible. During his life his theological enemies brought scandalous accusations against him. "There's ay some water where the stirkie droons"; and I tried to please both sides with this poem, though I have my doubts about some of the ministers.

ROAD TO CARRINGTON

A teen-age poem in English in the Georgian style, that by its clear descriptions took a fancy of the Training College rural students. Nobody in 1922, God help their simple souls, knew any better, for T. S. Eliot had just "arrived"; Auden, Spender, and MacNeice were still lisping numbers in short pants, and the "Movement" poets were immobile larvae.

SNAWDON WOOD

In the Twenties I often camped in midwinter with friends in the Lammermuirs and Moorfoots. This poem describes the actual scene and happenings on an unearthly moonlight December night in the sinister Danskine area. An inn-keeper here, centuries ago, murdered many guests before being convicted. The nunnery of Nunraw is now rebuilt but from its former ruins the superstitious often imagined they heard the "deid-bell". Danskine is the old name for Denmark: Danish settlers may have lived here.

94

TWAL OORS IN PARADISE

According to the Talmud, Adam and Eve were only twelve hours in Eden. This is quite commensurable with the Six Days of Creation. Indeed by a scientific time-scale the whole of human history only occupies seconds in the cosmic day. I have shown the capacity of the Scots tongue for encapsulating grand themes, at the expense of deflating them, of course. Scots, like Dutch, is an existentialist's or pragmatist's medium.

STISHIE AT THE STEAMIE

Edinburgh has its own humour which is quite different from Glasgow's. As an Auld Reekie man, (though also not unacquainted with the humour of Dunbarton in my childhood), I here present a picture of East Edinburgh at the grass-roots. The "Regent" was a picture-house, "Beggie" the familiar name of Dr. Begg's Buildings, (where I had many friends). Beggie is now demolished but had been an improved housing block, by the social reformer Dr. Begg in 1830; there being one water-closet for every four families, a big improvement then.

None of the personal names are other than fictitious, in a commotion which is equally mythological.

WHITEST PEBBLE ON SANNA'S SHORE

Like Alastair Mackie, whose poem-sequence "At the Heich Kirk-yaird" was dedicated to me, I am enthralled by Ardnamurchan, which, once teeming with clansfolk and cattle, was totally ravished after Culloden and has never recovered. I wrote this lyric recently (1978), its inspiration being similar to the earliest love-lyric in this selection, "Lowden Lass" (1921).

POSTSCRIPT TO "ON CEMENTING LEVEL THE STABLE FLOOR, Etc."

On Hogmanay 1978 a tempestuous storm undermined and washed away the old Stable. This suggests a final verse.

> Neptune contemptuous of both man and horse
> Rased their memorial in a tour de force
> And at the dictate of the merest whim
> Levelled alike Yahoo and Houyhnhnm